Poems for
ENCOURAGEMENT,
Words for THE HEART

Poems for ENCOURAGEMENT, Words for THE HEART

KEVIN MAST

TATE PUBLISHING
AND ENTERPRISES, LLC

Published by Tate Publishing & Enterprises, LLC
127 E. Trade Center Terrace | Mustang, Oklahoma 73064 USA
1.888.361.9473 | www.tatepublishing.com

Tate Publishing is committed to excellence in the publishing industry. The company reflects the philosophy established by the founders, based on Psalm 68:11,
"The Lord gave the word and great was the company of those who published it."

Book design copyright © 2016 by Tate Publishing, LLC. All rights reserved.
Cover design by Samson Lim
Interior design by Caypeeline Casas

Published in the United States of America

ISBN: 978-1-68187-388-6
1. Poetry / Subjects & Themes / Inspirational & Religious
2. Poetry / General
15.10.09

To my mom, Linda Mast,
who died on May 2, 2015, in a tragic car crash.
I will always remember your sweet spirit.

ACKNOWLEDGMENTS

I would like to first thank the Holy Spirit who prompted me to get a pen and write these poems. If the Holy Spirit would not have done this, then my emotions would have not have gotten out, I would have felt depressed, and have a broken heart. I thank Jesus for being God, who is feeling my pain, praying for me, and is crying for me so that I can be set free. I thank the Father who has always loved me with a perfect love.

I would like to thank Rick Joyner. The books that he wrote are mostly about dreams he had, and reading them has created in me a hunger to set up in my life the expectation of having my own dreams and vision, so that I can love God more and have a fresh perspective on my own calling.

I would like to thank John Eckhardt, an apostle and author. Many of his books have equipped Christians with tools to be set free from demonic attacks through the acts of declaring and decreeing the Word of God.

I would like to thank C. S. Lewis for so many things including writing the *Chronicles of Narnia*, the *Screwtape Letters*, and *a Grief Observed*. The Screwtape Letters has helped me understand myself so much and helped me cope with the fact that I have seemingly gone through worse trials than the average person. *A Grief Observed* taught me to confront my own emotions, and taught me to be honest with God about how I feel about life, even if it means complaining to Him so that I can get rid of my negative feelings.

I would like to thank preacher and intercessor, Corey Russell, of International House of Prayer (IHOP). Music has teamed up with his prayers and it is an awesome anointing. For the last month, I only have been listening to him because he has knowledge and urgency these past days that I desire to possess.

I would like to thank the Fort Wayne Vineyard. They prophesied over my life for over thirty minutes and that has been the foundation of my faith, warning me of my very difficult trials and talking about the faithfulness to God in my life. Most of the words given to me are just beginning to happen some twenty years after they were given.

I would like to thank Glen and Linda Mast, my father and mother. They always believed in me even when I went off in the deep end.

I would like to thank my uncle, Harold Mast, who used to be a pastor. He is always a phone call away to talk about my troubles and victories.

I would like to thank Gary Forgey, my mentor, who is always embracing me with a warm lingering hug. He always encourages me and saw potential in my poems when I gave him a copy of one.

I would like to thank Alex Sortman, my other mentor, the man of God, who always taught me to first listen to God and then pray what is on God's heart when praying for an individual.

I would like to thank Life Gate Church that has always embraced me these past 12 years I have been going there. I am blessed there. I am so thankful for the forty minutes of worship, and the congregation encouraging me to pray for one another when there is a need while worship is going on.

The last person I would like to thank is my pastor, Andy Weil, who especially knows what to say at crucial times. He has always seen potential in me and has always thanked me for using my spiritual gifts.

CONTENTS

Foreword.. 13

Introduction... 15

God's Shining Tears of Concern 19

Shelter Me, Lord 23

Thanks 25

Living the Best You Can Each Day 27

The Light.. 31

Knocked Down Again 33

Dancing for the Audience of One................... 35

Soaring 36

Can We Soar in Crisis?.................................. 39

Pleasant Thoughts.. 42

Part I: God on Trial 45

Part II: Redemption...................................... 47

Behold, I Stand at the Door and Knock 49

Taking Paths to the Good Life 52

Inspired by Eph. 2:10 (Amplified Version)

The Way, the Truth, and the Life 54

Inspired by John 14:6

Trust and Worship When Feeling Perplexed and
Unable to Find a Way Out 56

Inspired by 2 Cor. 4:8 (Amplified Version)

Where Is the God of Elijah? 59

I Love Life 61

Open My Eyes to Your Faithfulness 63

Sacred Anointing Oil, Pour Over Me 65

Disarming Satanic Power 69

Equip Me, Lord 73

Wrestling God 75

Inspired by Gen. 32

Elisha, Man of God, Who Thrived in Crisis 77

Am I Worthy of the Spirit and Favor of Joseph? 81

Can Your Dry Bones Live? 85

Based on Ezek. 37, Rom. 4:17

God, Please Visit Me 87

FOREWORD

This collection of poems is something you will want to keep on hand, readily available, to refer to again and again. They come to us out of the depth of the heart, for they were born out of the crucible of life. We might never walk the same path that Kevin has walked; however, every one of us has our own pilgrimage from which we can identify with him. If we are learning and growing, we also have our crucible from which that occurs. Even though our walk is different, we can be empowered, encouraged, enriched, instructed by another who speaks from the heart, sharing their pilgrimage of discovery.

Kevin is among those of us who have had everything stripped from us except our relationship with the Lord. You will readily note that even that was many times brought into question, similar to that of the author of the Psalms of the Old Testament of the Holy Scriptures. The invitation is here in these pages to—also like him, with that relationship as a central focus—discover a resolve to the dilemmas that life sends our way.

These expressions from the heart have emerged out of Kevin's walk for the last decade—first a trickle, and then more frequently. These were not written to be compiled into a book. They emerged along the way out of the depth of life's challenges. Kevin has shared them as they emerged with those of us close to him. That circle has continued to broaden until it included the group of poets that he meets with on a regular basis in his hometown—for mutual support and encouragement that can take place only among peers. It just seems the time is here now to publish what is currently in hand, knowing full well that this flow will continue, for writing from the heart is a natural part of Kevin's life.

While in the midst of publishing this collection of writings, a major loss occurred for Kevin: the sudden death of his mother. His pilgrimage of the past years had prepared him to face this loss and move forward, discovering a healthy resolve of the grief that so suddenly came upon him.

Being the son of my younger brother, I had the pleasure of watching Kevin grow from infancy. Now here during these adult years, it has been an honor to be a part of his life's journey. May you as well benefit from Kevin's pilgrimage through time spent with these pages.

Rev. Harold L. Mast

INTRODUCTION

Throughout my life, I have faced many trials. I thought that I could never prosper because of the storm in life that I was going through. I have faced a lot of heartaches, and my poems reveal this. They are about me being a brave man cutting my heart open, revealing to God how I felt then receiving from Him and Jesus the inner healing.

I had to let out my negative feelings about how in the crevasses of my heart I felt about Him, and I did this through my poetry. Then, like David from the Bible, I proclaimed God's faithfulness throughout my life. Because of me admitting to God how I felt about Him and the intense desire for Him to change my heart, today I can rejoice in God's faithfulness. These poems are my journey to freedom and the tremendous amount of joy in finding that freedom in Jesus Christ.

All of these poems are spirit-led. I did not just sit down to write a poem. There was always a stirring in my spirit that I better get a pen and jot down my thoughts. I believe the Holy Spirit guided my thoughts in a somewhat similar way the Bible was written. I would say my poems are Bible-digested containing its principles.

Months later after writing these poems, I usually sit down and reread them. I am amazed how much wisdom they contain and how much they help me in my own struggles. Five of the poems are dear to my heart since I memorize them and present them in a dramatic fashion in front of churches. I am reminded how these poems were guided by the hand of God.

I challenge you that if you are struggling with life and need a pick-me-up, these poems are for you. They are for everyone but are designed specifically for those who question God's faithfulness with the intent of finding a faithful God. My heart is not necessarily to make money off of these poems. They are designed to set the captive free so that people can have a closer walk with God. The invitation is given. Come and enjoy these pieces of written artwork and see your spirits soar.

GOD'S SHINING TEARS
OF CONCERN

Lord, bend Your ear to my cry.
Stretched to the limit, I sigh.
A deep longing in my depths to be free.
Please, please have mercy on me.

A compassionate God You are is Your claim.
Is that true or an idealism that is lame?
Though at times, I think You don't care.
Your body on the cross is Your love to
    me You wanted to share.

God, do You know what would make my day?
To see You weep over my affair and
    say, "I am here to stay".
I see it now, in my crisis, You are concerned about me.
I now feel it deep in my heart to be.

Since You care, my faith is blazing.
This love is above amazing.
As our spirits embrace,
I can run with gusto this life's race.

It actually doesn't matter if the obstacle is there or gone.
I am already three-fourths.
My attitude is beaming with trust.
My God in this trial is the judge that is just.

Those shining tears of compassion are all I need.
Faith, hope, and love are growing in my heart,
    produced by His weeping seed.
My entire life now is to please my Heavenly Father above.
Through Him, when trials come I will
    have peace like a dove.

SHELTER ME, LORD

I am not strong enough
For a head on collision
Against this devil's force.
I know it is the enemy who is attacking me,
But power in myself is futile.

Shelter me, Lord, against this storm.
Honesty and obedience are my weapons,
But only You are more powerful against this attack.
Shelter me against this storm.

My foot is slipping.
I cry out in desperation,
But my crier is losing its power.
My heart is fully slung
As it is bleeding uncontrollably.
Only in You do I put my trust,
But my trust in You is fading away.

When there are no more options,
I cry out, 'how long?"
But that has been my stance for so long.
Have mercy,
But I believe You have forgotten to be merciful.

All of a sudden, the storm is over.
My stance hasn't changed.
All of a sudden, I am standing on this mountain.
I am an overcomer.
It doesn't make sense.
I gave up on life.
I even gave up on You.

It is all about You.
Nothing about me,
I did nothing but obey.
You just restored me
So now I can act in confidence.
Thank You for sheltering me
When I believed You didn't care.

THANKS

You are truly one of a kind,
In trying to help me out of this bind.
Friends like you are hard to find.

When I am around you, my heart is free.
I can express how I feel and be me.
You can also be yourself and you will see,

That I am one of the most understanding guys.
I am not full of lies.
I pray that when you're around me,
    you will experience highs.

When we are together, you will feel beautiful inside,
Because your beauty, inside and outside, you can't hide.
It shines and I hope you feel comfortable in me to confide.

I have so much to offer you.
I will show you a love that is true.
And demonstrate a respect every girl is due.

I will not preach or condemn,
But gently lead you to Him,
So that your light will no longer be dim.

You see, our friendship is an ultimate joy.
You have helped establish my manhood,
     I am no longer a boy.
I am as excited as a child with a new toy.

I truly want to spend quality time,
With you, I would step on a dime—
Just to hear me chime.

I love you with a gentle love.
I hope when you are around me you feel as free as a dove.
Thanks for being here for me and
     remember, I am here for you too.

Best friends forever.

LIVING THE BEST
YOU CAN EACH DAY

Do what you know to do.
Don't be rebellious. It might seem like
    you are stuck in the mud
And you are spinning and going nowhere.
You got to.
You got to.
Do what your heart tells you to do.
Laziness is out of the question.

But if you don't have enough strength,
Don't beat yourself up.
Be content with each day.
Never look down on yourself.
Especially if you know that you could not have done more,
If you couldn't have done more for the day.

If you feel like giving up,
rest.
But don't let yourself get to that point,
That point of deep depression.
But if by chance you find yourself there,
seek help!
Cry out. Cry out with your heart.
And say with the depths of it, "I need help!"
Help is waiting for you.

Life can be rough.
At times, it gives you a whipping
And knocks you all over the place,
Endure the pain and get back up.
You will get your reward
If you stay true and your heart doesn't condemn.

There is something about living the fullest of each day.
The journey of life is never arrived in a
    twenty-four-hour period.
Put your foot in front of the other.
Relax and have fun.
In the fullness of time, reflect
And see the awesome progress you have made.
Those things that used to upset you
Now fill your life with joy.

THE LIGHT

If your heart has been ripped to pieces
And you see no light,
Only darkness engulfs you,
All you do is barely stay afloat,
While everybody tells you that you are
    doing something wrong
When there is not a rebellious bone in your body.

That is when He has the opportunity
    to come to your rescue.
All He wants is your honesty before
    Him about your crisis,
And the necessity of Him to shine in your life
    He wants to feel.
When you start praising Him with a pure heart,
He uses the most powerful searchlight
    you could ever imagine,
Which exposes the dooming entanglements
    that have been haunting your life.

For the sake of His Name, He will rescue you.
You proclaim Him as Father.
He has marked you as a prized king.
You are royalty.
You just went through a bump in the road.

After He has shown His light into your life,
You have become a lighthouse to this hurting generation.
You then are able to expose the jagged rocks that
Would have shipwrecked other people's lives.
All of your previous darkness and
    gloom now has meaning.

You know by experience how it feels
    to have a troubled heart
And how empty life can be at times.
Your powerful light leads people to the true light.
You find the huge joy of satisfaction of
    rescuing so many people.

In light of this, you thank Him for
    every trial and tribulation
That prepared you to be the hero you now are.
Think of how many people now see the light,
Because you endured the darkness.
What an awesome God we serve.

KNOCKED DOWN AGAIN

Why?! Why?! Why?!
This pattern always happens.
I get up from a nasty fall,
And then someone knocks me down in judgment.
Don't they understand they are killing my spirit?
Don't they care about me?
And worse off, He doesn't seem to care.
I know this can't be true.
But sometimes it feels like
He enjoys it when I am knocked down.
He is supposed to be my helper.
Not my mocker.

Then the light comes on.
Unless I am broken,
I can't truly be thankful.
I realize there is someone evil fighting against me.
I learn to abhor this gruesome foe.
I want it gone from me with a passion.
I want it gone so badly
That I don't care that I am laid out flat on the floor.
I know that these nasty falls are destroying what I despise.
Fallen states of mind are never pleasurable, or are they?
I am learning to trust Him in sufferings.
Never suffer needlessly.
But enjoying being knocked down

Because it is killing my harmful self,
The self that would have ended up killing me.

Being knocked down has new meaning.
I am no longer fighting it.
It has helped me.
It produces new stamina.
Oh the joy, of my sinful nature being knocked down.
So, I can stand in freedom.

DANCING FOR THE AUDIENCE OF ONE

Dancing in the streets
Thus my anxious thought retreats.
My spirit is soaring.
Such a thrill, far from boring.

I jam and groove to the beat.
His presence comes into my being as a fiery heat.
A new sense of freedom descends down,
Clothed with a sensation of praise, wearing this gown.

I am of course not dancing for any human's recognition.
But to get closer to His heavenly position.
Closer to His Glory,
That is my ultimate goal and story.

I want to dance with Father God in step with His feet
And feel His glorious heartbeat.
I could do this all night
As my emotions rise to a new height.

Why for the world would I dance?
No way do I want to flirt with hell and take that chance.
Nothing compares to getting down into His peace.
Thank goodness His presence goes on
　　　and on, it will never cease.

SOARING

I looked up at the clear-blue sky
Then I saw it.
An eagle, and effortless it did fly.
I admired it with glee
Because the soarer seemed so free.

Could I do that?
I know I can't fly, but what about my being?
I want to fly because my spirit is so flat.
Why couldn't my emotions soar?
So many people had grounded me and
    my confidence they did tore.

Once I had joy,
But jealous men had shot at my emotions.
My feelings, they thought was a toy.
The pain, they had caused so much pain,
So bad that I symbolically couldn't stand without a cane.

But know I am in awe
Of the thought of my inner self flying.
I want to feel like I am ten feet tall.
I had been grounded for too long.
I wanted to be so high, so that no one could
    stop me not even King Kong.

I knew that soaring was a choice.
I had to force my thoughts to coincide with joy
So I bellowed, "I will fly" with a powerful voice.
The negative emotions left that is true
As I closed my eyes and imagine I was
    flying toward the blue.

How jubilant I now feel.
My feet may still be on the ground
But my spirit is flying, that is the deal.
I know trials are here
But I know now that I can jump over
    them bounding like a deer.

I am getting used to soaring
Much better than pouting.
A continual grievous heart is wrong and boring.
I have overcome lots of things.
It is now easier to allow a heart that sings.

So up, up, up, I go.
No greater thrill in life
As I abolish negative grievousness as my foe.
Now in this world I don't have a care,
So try to determine to let yourself soar
    like an eagle is a dare.

Son

CAN WE SOAR IN CRISIS?

I looked intently at the book.
I did a double take.
I couldn't believe what my eyes saw.
Could my spirit actually soar?
It said I could go beyond soaring.
Mount up with wings as eagles?

But this couldn't be true!
I guess there was a time I soared.
But as I was soaring, a man thought
    I literally was an eagle.
He took a gun and shot at me.
All because I could fly and he couldn't.
The bullet went straight to my heart.
It didn't kill me, but my emotions
    have never been the same.
The pain, the pain, the pain of my bleeding heart.
But, for some reason, the wounds did heal.
And I did become stronger because of them.

And then came the storms.
You all know that birds don't fly when it is raining.
Flying in storms is another matter.
Attempting to fly in storms are just like crisis.
I hate both of them.

I can't fly in a storm!
But something inside of me said I could.

One of the biggest problems I have is becoming weary.
I just don't have the energy to get done
    what needs to be done.
And God, You expect me to fly when I am exhausted!
But there was something that was mentioned in that book
Something I forgot.
It said I had to wait on Him.
Then I could mount up with wings as eagles.
Could God actually help me to soar when I am weary?
Just by being patient and wait on His voice and direction?

There are a million, zillion reasons why I should not soar,
But this book said I could.
I knew the book was above reason.
I wanted to at least give it a try.
I had been grounded too long with tears.
I deserve to fly.
I guess I will give it a try.
I awkwardly flap my wings.
All of a sudden, I do it.
My spirit is soaring.

Hear comes the jealous man with the gun.
A round of bullets fly at me.
This time, I am expecting it, and I easily dodge them.
Here comes the storms of life.
I exert myself a little and fly towards the sun
Far above my stormy life.
I am patient and wait for His dictations.

I am no longer tired.
I am no longer in control.
He is in control.
He controls the wind.
And with my heart, I trust Him to carry me,
I can't believe it!
The book is true!
I am an eagle mounting up to the Son.
I am happy—even in crisis.
It is far better than flying with the eagles.
I am soaring with the angels, just to glorify God.

PLEASANT THOUGHTS

I have never felt this joyous before!
Someone actually understands me.
Before I even have to speak a word,
You are there in my darkest hour of trial
And pick me off from my grief.

I always knew that God cared about me,
And I have been touched by His gentle compassions.
But I never knew that a human being can put
    out the fire of my burning heart.
These have been the best days of my life,
Filled with happiness I never knew existed.

I can't sleep at night.
Your pretty smile is always on my mind.
At the same time, I never had so much
    energy and zeal for life.
All I can meditate on is your spirit,
That wants to calm my storm.
No one has came as close to me as you have,
And you still care about me.

We don't have to talk or see each other.
There is such an excitement when I see
    your car parked outside
And I know you are home. I have felt your glorious spirit

And I know you have felt mine.
Remember, I am a warrior and you can lean on me.

I am an apple tree of the forest.
Come. Sit by my side.
And eat from my fruit that is sweet to the taste.
I will strengthen you with apples (inspired
    by Song of Sg. 2:2–6).

You are a gift sent from God.
No matter what happens in the future,
I will always be close to your heart as a friend,
Who loves people
And desires to bring the best out of them.
My deepest gratitude to you.

PART I
GOD ON TRIAL

Frustrated, God, where are You?
Another day of nothingness.
When will the darkness end?
As the grasp of suicide seems inevitable.
I don't want to die.
Just want to be set free from this injustice.
Nobody understands the difficulties I go through.
I search all day—Nothing.
What about Your Word?
Never will I leave you—as You say.
It's up to You.
You said My sheep will hear Your voice.
I am Your sheep eternally.
What happened to Your Providence?
Yet, I will praise You.
How can I praise someone who seems
    not to care about my life?
You said the very hairs of my head
    are numbered—so what?
I would rather feel Your peace and protection.
So many people judged me in the past.
Judging because they know it all.
Only if people could see my heart and determination
And understand my handicaps,
I long to abide with You, God.

God, why is it so hard to know Your will in life?
I pant for Your heart for my life.
Are You faithful and true as You say You are?
Or a person who makes a lot of empty promises?

PART II
REDEMPTION

God, I understand now.
Pain has its own purpose.
Who am I to doubt Your Sovereignty?
You are faithful and true as You say You are.
You are concerned about my handicaps.
Thank You for installing patient endurance inside of me.
I know now that You want me to trust You, be faith.
I am so thankful that we can approach
     Your throne of grace
In our time of need.
You desire me to go out and help the troubled heart
And say, "Let the afflicted hear and rejoice."
Your love endures forever.
Thank You for breathing Your breath of life into me.

BEHOLD,
I STAND AT THE DOOR
AND KNOCK

Softly and gently, it was heard first.
Then, it grew louder this outburst.
Sounded like someone banging on my door.
An unexplained chill ran through my core.

Questions flooded my mind.
Could my unexpected visitor be mean or kind.
Then, I heard His voice.
My heart did leap, it did rejoice.

For on the door's other side.
Was the One I longed to be with and abide.
It was Jesus Christ my Savior and Lord.
He was the One my entire life adored.

What a joy to have the person at my door that I trust!
Other people came and treated my life like dust.
I learned not to let everyone in.
Past mistakes, letting people whose lives were full of sin.

Now the moment I had been waiting for.
I knew my first glimpse of Him, my spirits would soar.
But it happened before I opened the door,
A rush of energy knocked me to the floor.

The energy was His intense love.
Wave after wave of His electrifying
    love set me free as a dove.
My thoughts, *Heaven couldn't be any better than this.*
His spirit and mine felt like they did kiss.

Then I saw a tear fall from His eye.
What could make my King sad, I asked why?
He regained His composure and spoke with a gentle tone.
I created mankind for me but for the
    most part they leave me alone.

Someone actually opened the door when I knocked.
When people find me out, they keep their doors locked.
They want nothing to do with me.
I am the one who could set them free.

I thought, *How could someone turn away the Glorious One.*
He is Father God's Glorious Son.
I hugged Him with passion.
He hugged back with fashion.

Then He gave me something to eat.
That was a glorious treat.
I never felt such love.
I had no idea such an awesome sensation
    could come from above.

I urge you to live in expectancy of a heavenly knock.
The clock does go ticktock, ticktock.
Time runs out if you don't answer the door.
You could spend eternity on the bottom floor.

That bottom floor is of course, hell.
This life is a test, don't fail.
Listen carefully to that knock from Jesus.
Opening that door confirms that He will never leave us.

TAKING PATHS
TO THE GOOD LIFE

Inspired by Eph. 2:10 (Amplified Version)

Meaningless, that was my life.
My emotions were full of strife.
I lived empty every day.
Nothing ever exciting came my way.

I realized I needed God-given dreams.
Joseph from the Bible had this, it seems,
So I asked God for this because I had needs,
"Since You did it for Joseph, why not give me leads?"

I wanted to know what would make me joy-filled.
Desiring my life to have the Holy Spirit approval sealed,
I wanted a scripture to come into my existence.
Faith on my part would be my assistance.

It said I could take a path of God prepared ahead of time
Then the good life would be mine.
I had to believe that God had a path of
    escape in every dilemma I got in,
No matter if I were in a heavy-duty sin.

Now each morning when I awake,
I want to hear from God which path to take.
What task does He want me to do to
    make me tick with gladness.
I know each day has a specific task,
    there is no more sadness.

I am living the good life and having visions,
Because I am obeying His decisions.
What an exuberant life I now live.
A joyous heart to God I now give.

THE WAY, THE TRUTH, AND THE LIFE

Inspired by John 14:6

Jesus said, "I am the way."
Way means a road one travels the
    Greek dictionary does say.
What does this mean?
Out of a tangled mess called life, there
    is God's path I have seen.

There are a lot of roads in life's race.
Inquire God which direction is right and keep in pace.
This requires a surrender of one's will.
Obedience to God's perfect objectives fits the bill.

Taking God's road of life produces peace.
Anxieties, fears, and worries will cease.
In God's shelter we can rest.
Though at times it gets intense, Jesus' path is life's best.

Traveling God's road means we will
    experience the truth of God's word.
A scripture in season causes us to fly free like a bird.
Intimacy and trust enables us to know
    what word to apply in life.

First we walk the road, which reveals
    the truth to end strife.

After these two attributes have been
    worked on, life is obtained.
This means the joy of life has been sustained.
Satan comes to destroy us he will try.
We can tell him bye-bye.

Since God's road we love,
God will look down from above
And His truth will be in our being.
The love of this life we will be seeing.

TRUST AND WORSHIP
WHEN FEELING PERPLEXED
AND UNABLE
TO FIND A WAY OUT

Inspired by 2 Cor. 4:8 (Amplified Version)

Sometimes in life we are perplexed and
    are unable to find a way out.
It is wrong to be given to despair and pout.
It is all about our perception.
Satan wants to make us think that God
    doesn't care, it is his deception.

Hope deferred makes the heart sick
But a longing fulfilled is what makes us tick.
Hope in God because He doesn't disappoint us.
Sometimes, it seems like He does but we have to trust.

So what do we do when life is more than we can handle.
We are on holy ground so symbolically
    take off each sandal.
As we humble ourselves before God, be in awe.
Our sinful nature crucified and His nature in
    us makes us feel like we're ten feet tall.

He is in control and loves us servants.
We have to pray with laments.
When we are meek, He uses His strong right hand
To open the door of heaven, so we take the land.

WHERE IS THE GOD OF ELIJAH?

Where is the God of Elijah?
What does this mean?
I'll tell you a tale straight from the good book.
This question will answer every financial need.
It's about obeying God and trusting Him.
Trusting Him as provider, not just trusting your provision.

Elijah obeyed God who said it wouldn't rain.
This command had the potential to harm him.
But God sent him a raven to feed him bread and meat.
He drank from a brook, but oh no,
The brook dried up.

It looks like his financial needs won't be met.
Then a profound statement is made.
God commanded a widow to feed him.
Elijah trusted God for his needs, not just his provision.

Bounds and bounds of miracles were
        performed through Elijah.
This poem does not have space to provide them.
Let's jump forward to Elisha.
Elijah mentored Elisha.
Elisha followed him through thick and thin.

Elijah and Elisha came to an immovable obstacle.
They couldn't pass through it, unless God showed up.
The obstacle was the Jordan River.
It represents any obstacle in your life.
Elijah took the mantle, and the Jordan parted.

Jumping forward in the tale again.
Elijah is taken to heaven, leaving behind his mantle.
Elisha picks it up and approaches the
        Jordan River, alone this time.
He asks the question that can change your life.
Where is the God of Elijah? And it parted.

I serve the same God Elijah served.
My obstacle, the Jordan River, will
        part if I'm in God's will.
If I am obedient to God, He must meet my financial need.
The next time a "Jordan River" is in front of you.
Ask, Where is the God of Elijah?
And experience the peace that passes all understanding.

I LOVE LIFE

Torment. Torment. Torment.
Is there any escape from this torment?
There is a pin in my brain,
That makes thinking impossible.
I thought I tried everything.
Prayer, much prayer, but to no avail.
Why can't someone place their hands on me
And zap a healing touch to restore my injured head?
I want it, and I want it now.

Then understanding comes to my soul.
God is working integrity in my life through these trials.
Following God's path is the only escape.
For me it is a process, not a microwave fixin'.
Slowly, but surely, I find truths from His word to cope.

Hopefully, now I have found the missing link
To drive the torment away.
Every time I feel the presence of pain,
I say to myself, "I love life."
At first it is just artificial words
Then it becomes a part of my being,
And it leaves.
I now genuinely enjoy life.
Now when the pain comes,

I thank God for being born.
Pain can't stop a thankful heart.
Now I can honestly say, "I love life."

OPEN MY EYES
TO YOUR FAITHFULNESS

Open my eyes to Your faithfulness to me
In a life where it seems You are nowhere to be.
An account I need to take,
Where You have helped me for my sake.

You have been faithful in many ways.
I have been fed all of my days.
I always had a roof over my head.
Never had I been without a bed.

Clothes I have had always to wear.
Never did they possess a tear.
Never have I been without a drink.
Running water always came from the sink.

I have always desired Your direction in life.
You're faithful, even cutting through the
        Amazon forest with a machete knife.
Yes, I am walking Your path
In order to escape the enemy's wrath.

Yes, my life has been protected
Because it is Your way I have selected.
Let me experience in my heart
Your faithfulness as You block the devil's dart.

I now experience Your complete faithfulness as real.
Why I doubted, I don't know what was the deal.
Let me see more and more
Your faithfulness so my spirit can soar.

SACRED ANOINTING OIL,
POUR OVER ME

O, Lord thank You for making
Everyone who serves You as priests.
That means we have access to the sacred
Anointing oil in which only the priest
        had in the Old Testament.
I know that if we ask for this,
You will judge us more strictly.
But it is the desire of my heart
To be holy in Your sight.
There is no other way,
        To true peace and happiness.

Let Your sacred anointing oil pour over my life.
I am so desperate for You.
I need You in the good times and the bad times.
I long for Your oil of gladness and joy.

Cover me, the temple of the Holy Ghost
With the sacred anointing oil.
My heart needs to enter into
The most holy place.
To comfort me from this hideous storm,
Equip me for every good work.
Only in Your presence, O God,
Can I experience true freedom.

All the way from the top of my head
   to the bottom of my feet,
Sacred anointing oil, pour over me.

(Jas. 3:1, Rev. 1:6, Exod., 30:22–33, Isa. 61:3, and Ps. 45:7)

DISARMING SATANIC POWER

Demons, you dare attack me.
Uh, uh, uh.
You shall be annihilated.
You show your ugly face.
I will call on the name of my God.
Do you know what He will do?
He shall strike you in the jaw.
He shall knock the teeth out of your mouth.
What do you think about that, demons?

Chorus
Arise O Lord,
Show Your glory and power.
Your mighty right hand will crush the enemy.

Rulers of darkness, why are you so stupid in attacking me?
Do you know what I will do?
I shall beat you as fine as dust.
I will laugh and mock you,
Because I know my authority in Christ.
When my precious Jesus died on the cross,
He made an open display of my enemies.
Now, I will praise my King.
Jesus, You are my victor.

Come on principalities of evil.
Raise the war cry and expect your doom.
Prepare for battle and be shattered.
Prepare for battle and be shattered.
Device your strategy and it will fail.
Propose your plan, and it will not stand.
For God is with us
No matter what direction you shall turn,
My Jesus will beat the living daylights out of you.

Out of nowhere,
The Lord will come out with His sword.
What sword are we talking about?
We are talking about His fierce, great, and powerful sword.
Leviathan is a demonic sea monster.
One of the strongest demonic forces ever created,
Javelins are like straw.
But the fierce sword of the Lord
Will penetrate and kill the almighty Leviathan.

(Ps. 3:7, 2 Sam. 22:38–43, Ps. 2:4, Col. 2:15,
    Isa. 8:9–10, Isa. 27:1, Job 41, Ps. 74:13–14)

"The Lord GOD hath given me
the tongue of the learned,
that I should know how to speak
a word in season to him that is weary:
he wakeneth morning by morning,
he wakeneth mine ear to hear as the learned."

-Isaiah 50:4

EQUIP ME, LORD

Lord, I seek Your face
As I come boldly to Your throne of grace.
There is an area in my life where I am lacking
In order to be better person, I need Your backing.

You see, it is Your thoughts I want to know.
Without hearing them I can't do Your will, this is so.
I don't only want to do what I want to do.
Wanting to conform myself to the new
    creation that comes from You.

Not only to become a better person but to
    give others Your words of insight.
I want to point people to Your light.
The necessity of hearing Your voice and
    not just giving my opinion.
My words must come from Your heart
    so they can have dominion.

Dominion over what oppresses them
So they can be set free and turned into a gem.
Lord, I want to be used by You
Because when I am not doing Your
    heart's desire, I am blue.

Right now, I admit my spiritual deafness to Your will.
Helping other people out more
    effectively would be a thrill.
I know I could do so much more.
If I had a word from You, I could comfort
    and get to a bleeding heart's core.

All I want to do is make the world a better place.
God, consider my case.
Increase fellowship with me and speaking to me,
Not only for me but for others you see.

WRESTLING GOD

Inspired by Gen. 32

In Biblical times, a person's character
    is revealed in his name.
Jacob means deceiver—his identity was the same.
The birthright from his elder brother he did steal.
For some stew from his famished
    brother, that was the deal.

When his father Isaac was about to die,
Jacob tricked his father to bless him, he did lie.
He claimed to be his elder brother is what he said.
When his elder brother realized what had
    happened, he wanted Jacob dead.

For his life, Jacob does flee.
His relative Laban, he was supposed to find and see.
But before this, he had an encounter with the Lord.
This experience was so awesome he built
    an altar and the Lord he adored.

Angels ascending and descending a ladder to heaven's gate,
And a powerful message from heaven God did relate.
His descendants would be as numerous as the stars.
The same promise given to Father and
    Grandfather he heard from afar.

A life-changing experience was this dream.
He knew he wouldn't be murdered, it would seem.
Then he journeyed and Laban he did find.
Then he fell in love with Laban's daughter,
     Rachel, she was one of a kind.

Then Laban tricked him,
Probably caused by Jacob's previous life of sin.
Now the deceiver became deceived.
He fled from Laban, he did leave.

Desiring to be changed, he wrestled a man,
     believed to be God, all night.
He fought with all of his soul and all his might.
"Change my character, change my name," he did say.
His new name, Israel, means to fight with God
     and is what he is called to this day.

Personally, I am not satisfied where I am at now.
My whole being to the Lord, I want to bow.
I am wrestling God to change my name.
I want God's destiny and mine be one
     page, that is the same.

I hunger for a closeness with God I
     haven't experienced yet.
I long to go deeper with Him and
     reach a whole new depth.
I cling to God's protection and peace,
Desiring warmth from Him that will never cease.

ELISHA, MAN OF GOD, WHO THRIVED IN CRISIS

When crisis comes our way,
Most of us don't know what to say.
We throw our hands up in the air,
And say life is a bear.

Elisha, man of God, does not do this.
He handled many crisis with a bliss.
No matter what way his problems came,
He operated the way that is always the same.

Crisis One.
People in a city had water that was bad
They couldn't drink it and that was sad.
Elisha asked for a bowl and for some salt.
The water turned pure, the diseased water came to a halt.
Crisis One Solved.

Crisis Two.
Creditors came to collect money from a prophet's wife.
They said they would take away her
    sons, now that is a strife.
The widow said all she had was a jar of oil.
She did what Elisha said, she was loyal.

She went around and collected from
    her neighbors' empty jars.
The result—the sons did not have to be slaves,
    being worse off than behind bars.
She poured oil she had in the empty
    jars and the oil didn't stop.
Of every jar she had, the oil came to the top.

She sold the oil and paid off her debts.
She even had extra money that she had kept.
Again when crisis hits Elisha, he thrives.
He is better than a cat with nine lives.
Crises Two Solved.

Crisis Three.
A loved boy is dead.
Elisha stretched himself on the corpse, he was led.
The boy sneezes 7 times and opens his eyes.
The boy's mother glorifies God and cries.
Crisis Three solved.

Crisis Four.
Nahaam had leprosy and wanted to be cured.
He wanted his skin to be pure.
Elisha tells him to go to the Jordan River
    and seven times take a dip.
The leprosy falls off, from his life it did skip.
Crisis Four Solved.

Crisis Five.
The company of prophets was in the
    woods cutting down trees.
As a man swung his ax, the axehead flees
Into the water it is lost.
He said that ax was borrowed, what a heavy cost.

Elisha throws a stick in the river and the axehead floats.
Elisha never did gloat, he never boasts.
He gave glory to God for His power
And left a taste in the devil's face that is sour.
Crisis Five Solved.

Crisis Six.
A prophet throws poisonous gourds into a pot.
The stew seemed no good was the stew's lot.
No fear.
Elisha puts flour in the pot, the food then tastes dear.
Crisis Six Solved.

Crisis Seven.
There was a hundred hungry people with a little food.
Only twenty loaves of barley baked, it
    was time for a miracle mood.
No way could that feed everyone, Elisha's servant thought.
But they had leftovers because the Word
    of the Lord Elisha sought.
Crisis Seven Solved.

Crisis Eight
An army surrounds Elisha and his servant.
The servant is terrified, his life was out of shape—bent.
Elisha prayed that the servant's eyes be open.
Angels surrounding them numbering far more than ten.

The angels blinded the army.
The servant does see
A great miracle that day.
Elisha always put his trust in God, in
    Him does his troubles are slain.
Crisis Eight Solved.

As this poem says, Elisha had several crisis.
He put his faith in God, His spirit still lives.
I cry out when crisis come my way
The word of the Lord I will say.

I will try my best to not worry.
Although I may be at first a little leery,
I will put my trust in Him and relax,
And not so much trust in the facts.

There is an avenue of escape.
I cut through the red tape.
Spirit of Elisha live in me.
When crisis hit, fear has to flee.

AM I WORTHY
OF THE SPIRIT AND FAVOR
OF JOSEPH?

Joseph went through some very difficult times.
Thrown in a pit and left for death by his brothers.
Sold into slavery,
Sent to jail while trying to remain pure.

None of these things seemed to slow him down.
He always remained true to God.
And it has shown throughout the land.
Pagan Potiphar saw that God's favor was always on him.
Joseph also was successful in all he did.
In jail, believe it or not, he was put in
     charge of all the inmates.

How did he do it?
That is my quest!
And I know it begins with God.

I am screaming for Joseph's favor.
In life, I have been thrown in a pit.
A pit where escape seems impossible.
I have been wrongly accused.
Symbolically being thrown in jail for no reason at all.

To the best of my knowledge, I have been true to God.
It is my turn to receive the same favor
    from God that Joseph had,
If God deems me worthy.

CAN YOUR DRY BONES LIVE?

Based on Ezek. 37, Rom. 4:17

Can these dry bones live?
The question to Ezekiel God gives.
You see God showed Ezekiel bones that are dry.
God wanted the bones to live, it was his cry.

He needed a man to stand in the gap,
A man of faith to give the bones a heavenly zap.
Ezekiel answered the question with,
    "Only You know, God".
Believing in the miraculous, Ezekiel
    only needed God's nod.

God told Ezekiel to speak forth dry
    bones into life—exchange.
Life entered the dry bones, now that is a radical change.
The miracle happened instantly.
God's glory always repeats itself consistently.

Think of what is happening in you.
Are there dry bones in you too?
Broken dreams, relationships that seem dead.
No way these dry bones can live, you have said.

Give God a chance to display His glory.
He will change the tune of your story.
God is full of resurrection power.
Your perspective is changed when you
    see on top of God's tower.

God wants you to have lots of dreams.
Dry bones to life, it seems.
Hear from Him
And reveal light where it was dim.

Call those things of God that are not as though they were
And experience a fire in your heart that will stir.
A life full of life where there was death, now that's hope.
With your problems, you will more than cope.

Yes, it is God's will.
Fear and anxieties will be still.
Speak life to your future. It has shown.
To release from your innermost being a groan.

A groan that says no to dry bones and lost potential.
A heart that is joyful in all your soul.
Dry bones to life in now my heartbeat.
I tell Satan face me and expect defeat.

GOD, PLEASE VISIT ME

In my heart, there is a yearning.
My soul cries out for this.
God, please visit me.
You visited people in the Bible.

(Chorus)
Why not me? Visit me.
Not for selfish reasoning.
Just to get closer to You,
And change history.

Your initial plan was communing with Adam and Eve.
Sin broke that fellowship.
But You gave Bible characters a taste of heaven
And visited them.

Noah and his family were all that were left,
Whose every thought were not wicked continuously.
You visited Noah
And told Noah to build an ark.

That ark preserved mankind
So that the human race would not be wiped out.
You trusted Noah.
Am I not trust-worthy enough?

You visited Abram, told him to pack up everything
And go out by faith to a new land.
Help me have that same faith in You.
To go where You tell me to go.

You visited Jacob when he needed help
As he was running for his life.
His brother, Esau, wanted him dead.
By this visitation, You brought peace that he would live.

There was a time Moses wasn't
        concerned about his mission
To set the Israelites free from captivity.
Then You visited him in the bush that would not burn.
This influenced Moses to lead the Israelites to freedom.

You visited Isaiah,
And he became conscious of his sin.
He was in awe of Your majesty
And said he wanted to be chosen to do God's will.

Paul was caught up in paradise
Up to the third heaven,
And he became the prominent writer
        of the New Testament.
Partly because You visited him.

You visited about every person in the Bible
Who did marvelous deeds for You.
I want to do great exploits for You.
The only way I know this is possible is if You visit me.